IT'S FUNNY WHEN YOU LOOK AT IT

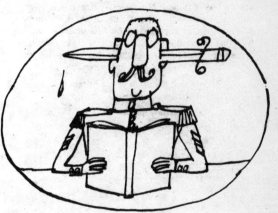

Poems & Pictures by
Colin West

Beaver Books

A Beaver Book
Published by Arrow Books Limited
62-65 Chandos Place, London WC2N 4NW

An imprint of Century Hutchinson Ltd

London Melbourne Sydney Auckland
Johannesburg and agencies throughout
the world

First published by Hutchinson Children's Books 1984
Beaver edition 1986

Text © Colin West 1984
Illustrations © Colin West 1984

Printed and bound in Great Britain by
Anchor Brendon Limited, Tiptree, Essex

ISBN 0 09 947650 9

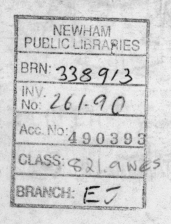

CONTENTS

The Human Race   9
Monsters and Monstrosities   21
Hopeless History   29
A Beginner's Guide to Nonsense   39
Fellow Creatures   51
Getting a Word in Edgeways   63
A Recipe for Disaster   73
From Here to Absurdity   83

It's funny when you look at it –

BACKWARDS

UPSIDE-DOWN

SIDEWAYS

Whichever way you look at it –
It's hard to wear a frown.

THE HUMAN RACE

Miss Feather and her Father

The father of Miss Feather
Cannot fathom her –
For the farther that Miss Feather
Feeleth from her far-off father,
Then the farther from her father
Fareth fair Miss Feather.

Alfie

Alfie studied art at college,
Crammed his head with useless knowledge,
Learned to paint upon wet plaster,
Thought he'd be a new Old Master.
Finding, though, no call for frescoes,
Alfie got a job at Tesco's.

Miranda

There's a girl I know – Miranda,
But I cannot understand her,
For she swapped her lovely panda
For a silly salamander.

Uncle Fergus

My Uncle Fergus eats beefburgers
Morning, noon and night.
He says it's hellish, but with relish,
Claims they taste all right.

Tom

They say that ignorance is bliss,
And Tom is living proof of this:
He's ignorant of many things,
And yet how merrily he sings,
Whilst others, wiser far than he,
Are gloomy to the nth degree.

The Lighthouse Keeper

I met the lighthouse
keeper's wife,
His nephew, niece,
and daughter;
His uncle and his
auntie too,
When I went 'cross
the water.

I met the lighthouse
keeper's son,
His father and his
mother;
His grandpa and his
grandma too,
His sister and his
brother.

I met the lighthouse
keeper's mate,
Who, running out
of patience,
Told me, 'The keeper's
gone ashore
To round up more
relations.'

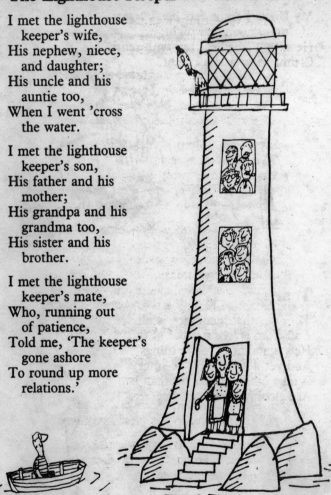

Christine Crump

Christine Crump is crunching crisps:
Cheese and onion, cheese and onion.
Christine Crump has crunched them.

Christine Crump is crunching crisps:
Smoky bacon, smoky bacon,
Cheese and onion, cheese and onion.
Christine Crump has crunched them.

Christine Crump is crunching crisps:
Ready salted, ready salted,
Smoky bacon, smoky bacon,
Cheese and onion, cheese and onion.
Christine Crump has crunched them.

Christine Crump is crunching crisps:
Curry flavour, curry flavour,
Ready salted, ready salted,
Smoky bacon, smoky bacon,
Cheese and onion, cheese and onion.
Christine Crump has crunched them.

Christine Crump is crunching crisps:
Salt and vinegar, salt and vinegar,
Curry flavour, curry flavour,
Ready salted, ready salted,
Smoky bacon, smoky bacon,
Cheese and onion, cheese and onion.
Christine Crump has crunched them.

Christine Crump is feeling sick . . .
Poor old Christine, poor old Christine,
She has indigestion.

My Sister Joan

I'm sad to say my sister Joan
Has confiscated my trombone,
And so, to get my *own* back,
Tonight, as she's tucked up in bed,
I'll play my violin instead . . .
Till I get my trombone back.

Stephen

Stephen sings into the nightfall,
And his voice is truly frightful,
Yet we deem it only rightful
To applaud and cry, 'Delightful!'

Miss Flibberty-Gibbet

Miss Flibberty-Gibbet, please tell me,
Pray, why do you act like you do?
You pedal your bicycle backwards
And wear an old hat from Peru.

Miss Flibberty-Gibbet, I've seen you,
When everyone else is in bed,
Frantically pedalling backwards,
Peruvian hat on your head.

Miss Flibberty-Gibbet, one morning,
I'll follow and see what you do,
When you pedal your bicycle backwards
And wear that old hat from Peru.

Miss Flibberty-Gibbet, I'll get you,
And that, as they say, will be that!
Then I'll pedal your bicycle backwards,
And wear your Peruvian hat.

Muriel

Muriel, Muriel,
You're oh so mercurial,
One moment you're up,
The next moment you're down.
Your moods are not durable,
You seem quite incurable –
For now you are laughing,
But soon you will frown.

Take It to Ned

If you've got a boat
That's unsinkable,
Take it to Ned,
He'll sink it.
It you've got a coat
That's unshrinkable,
Take it to Ned,
He'll shrink it.
If you've got a drink
That's undrinkable,
Take it to Ned,
He'll drink it.
But if you've got a thought
That's unthinkable,
Please keep it to yourself.

Rodney Reid

In his bathtub Rodney Reid is
Making quite a mess,
Thus disproving Archimedes'
Principle,* no less.

(Note the body in this case is
But a boy of four,
Yet the fluid it displaces
Covers all the floor.)

*When a body is immersed in water, its apparent loss of weight is
equal to the weight of the water displaced. So there!

Uncle Norman

My eccentric Uncle Norman
Always keeps his uniform on,
Even when he has a nap
Or goes to bed;
And he looks a funny fellow
In his coat of black and yellow,
With his traffic warden's cap
Upon his head.

I once asked him why he wore it,
And he answered, 'I adore it,
For it helps me sleep
Whilst counting traffic signs;
And I dream of parking meters,
Sporty chaps in their two-seaters,
And of booking them
On double yellow lines!'

Nicolo

'Can it be normal, Nicolo, to blow upon your
  piccolo
Beneath the roaring sea?
Tis rather odd behaviour, don't you agree,
  Octavia,
Don't you agree with me?'

'Not really, I think Nicolo is brave to blow his
  piccolo
Beneath the roaring sea.
This harmless eccentricity amuses me; Felicity,
Don't you agree with me?'

'Of course not! I think Nicolo is mad to blow his
  piccolo
Beneath the roaring sea.
Few hobbies could be loonier, don't you agree,
  Petunia,
Don't you agree with me?'

'Why, no! I'm sure that Nicolo is right to play his
  piccolo
Beneath the roaring sea.
'Tis rather odd behaviour for someone from
  Belgravia,
But still it's fine with me!'

An Understanding Man

I have an understanding
With an understanding man:
His umbrella I stand under
When I understand I can.

MONSTERS AND MONSTROSITIES

Petunia's Pet

Petunia's pet is a pet-and-a-half,
Some say it's a tapir, some say a giraffe.
Some say it is neither, some say it is both,
But Pet doesn't care and she's plighted her troth.

The Blunderblat

Until I saw the Blunderblat
I doubted its existence;
But late last night with Vera White,
I saw one in the distance.

I reached for my binoculars,
Which finally I focused;
I watched it rise into the skies,
Like some colossal locust.

I heard it hover overhead,
I shrieked as it came nearer;
I held my breath, half scared to death,
And prayed it might take Vera.

And so it did, I'm glad to say,
Without too much resistance.
Dear Blunderblat, I'm sorry that
I doubted your existence.

The Snorting Snorzus

How tiresome is the Snorting Snorzus!
No matter what, he just ignores us;
And should we manage one to capture,
He doesn't feel the *slightest* rapture.

How dare he be so apathetic,
Nonchalant and unathletic?
(Irritating all and sundry
With his snores so loud and thundery.)

O let's make out the Snorting Snorzus
Likewise unutterably bores us.
Henceforth we'll all relations sever,
And leave him well alone for ever!

Monstrous Imagination

'Mummy, can't you see the monster
Hiding by the curtain?'
'Why, Joseph dear, there's nothing there,
Of that I am quite certain.
The monster that you *think* you see
Within the shadows lurking,
Is your imagination, dear,
Which overtime is working.'

Thus reassured, Joe went to sleep;
His mother's explanation
Seemed only right: Beasts of the Night
Are mere imagination.
And sound his slumber was until
In dreams the monster met him.
Now Joe we'll miss, for last night his
'Imagination' ate him.

The Snoope

Upon the beauty of the Snoope
I must recite a sonnet;
As earthworms slither through the soil,
And poets prance upon it,
I've never seen another beast
That wears a bright blue bonnet.

Upon his head and hands and feet
He grows the finest bristles;
And as he goes upon his way,
He warbles and he whistles.
It's such a joy to watch him waltz
Between the thorns and thistles.

So to the beauty of the Snoope
I dedicate this ditty;
I hope I'll see another soon
In countryside or city.
Alas, till then, I can but wish
That I were *half* as pretty.

The Nippogriffinoctopus

Ted was left no time to wonder
What it was that dragged him under;
But I'll tell you what it was –
A Nippogriffinoctopus.

Perhaps 'tis all the same to Ted
As to what bit off his head:
Even if he'd chanced to glance it,
He'd not have managed to pronounce it.

The Furbelow

The Furbelow will eat your home,
From the floorboards to the rafters;
Then, having scoffed the furniture,
Will eat you up for afters.

The Woebegone and Woebetide

O woebetide you if upon
Your bed you find a Woebegone;
And woebegone you if beside
That beast there sits a Woebetide.

These beasts are often found in pairs,
There is no friendship quite like theirs;
They love each other, but it's true
They do not care for me or you.

So if by chance you come upon
The beast they call the Woebegone,
Be off! Or you'll end up inside
His only friend the Woebetide.

(And likewise, you should run and hide
If you should see a Woebetide –
Or else you might end up upon
The menu of the Woebegone.)

HOPELESS HISTORY

Nero

Nero, plump about the middle,
Played requests upon the fiddle.
The most engaging tune he played
Was for the local fire brigade.

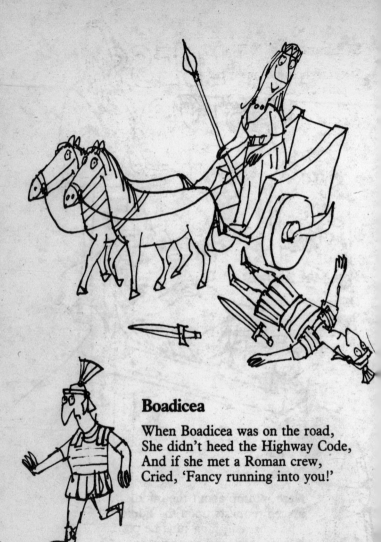

Boadicea

When Boadicea was on the road,
She didn't heed the Highway Code,
And if she met a Roman crew,
Cried, 'Fancy running into you!'

St Simeon

St Simeon could never be
A pillar of society;
And yet, for thirty years, upon
A pillar sat St Simeon.

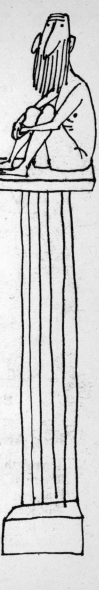

Peter the Hermit

On seeing a worm, it
Struck Peter the Hermit
As odd that such creatures
Should fascinate preachers.

King Arthur's Knights

King Arthur's knights were chivalrous
When sat around his table,
But even they were frivolous
Whenever they were able,
And in the moat at Camelot
They splashed about and swam a lot.

1066

Here's William of Normandy,
For battle he's apparelled,
And sailing off to Pevensey
To keep a date with Harold.

Waterloo

Said Napoleon at the start:
'I'll tear his every bone apart.'
Replied the Duke of Wellington:
'I'll *boot* his little skeleton.'

Columbus

Columbus very well knew that
The world was round, it wasn't flat,
And almost went hysterical
Just proving it was spherical.

Elizabeth I

Elizabeth the First, I hear,
Was quite a fussy queen,
And had a hot bath once a year
To keep her body clean.

Ivan the Terrible

Ivan the Terrible,
The first Russian Tsar,
Was just about bearable,
Till he went too far.

George Washington

George Washington chopped down a tree
And couldn't tell a lie;
When questioned by his father, he
Confessed, 'Yes, it was I.'

But as he handed back the axe,
He added in defence:
'Good training, sir, for lumberjacks
Or would-be presidents.'

A Survey of Sovereigns

William, William, Henry the First,
Stephen and Henry the Second;

Richard and John, sir, and Henry the Third,
Then one, two, three Edwards, 'tis reckoned.

Richard the Second and Henry the Fourth,
And Henrys the Fifth and the Sixth, sir;

Edward the Fourth and young Edward the Fifth,
Then Richard or Crooked King Dick, sir.

Henry the Seventh and Henry the Eighth,
Then Edward, then Mary was queen, sir.

Elizabeth, James, then Kings Charles One and Two,
(With Oliver Cromwell between, sir).

James, William & Mary, then following Anne,
Four Georges, one after another;

Then William, Victoria, Edward and George
To Edward, who said, 'Crown my brother.'

Einstein

Long years ago, nobody cared
That E was really mc^2.
Then Albert Einstein thought a bit,
And felt that he should mention it.

A BEGINNER'S GUIDE TO NONSENSE

Toboggan

To begin to toboggan, first buy a toboggan,
But don't buy too big a toboggan.
(A too big a toboggan is not a toboggan
To buy to begin to toboggan.)

Grandfather Clock

O grandfather clock, dear old grandfather clock,
How charming to hear is your tick and your tock;
So upright you stand day and night in the hall,
Your feet on the ground and your back to the
    wall.

Although I may grumble
    most mornings at eight,
When you chime, 'hurry up,
    or you're bound to be late,'
I'm grateful to greet you
    at five o'clock when
You chime, 'welcome home,
    nice to see you again.'

I think it is thoughtless
    when relatives speak
And rudely refer to you
    as an antique;
It also seems heartless
    when sometimes they say
You'd fetch a fair price
    at an auction one day.

I know that you're old
    and inclined to be slow,
But I hope that they never
    decide you should go.
How dull life would be
    if they took you away:
You give me much more
    than the time of the day.

Tout Ensemble

Paula pounds the grand piano,
Vera plays the violin,
Percival provides percussion
On an empty biscuit tin.
Connie plays the concertina,
Mervyn strums the mandolin;
When you put them all together –
They make one almighty din.

Custard

I like it thin without a skin,
My sister likes it thicker.
But thick or thin, when tucking in,
I'm noisier and quicker.

Water Skier

I'd like to be a water skier,
But I'm a little wobbly
When wearing skis and people tease
My knees for being knobbly.

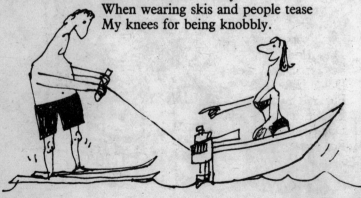

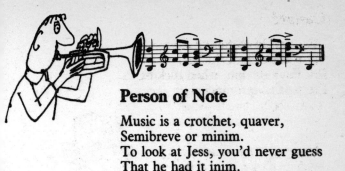

Person of Note

Music is a crotchet, quaver,
Semibreve or minim.
To look at Jess, you'd never guess
That he had it inim.

Eric, Eric, Go Away

Eric, Eric, go away,
Don't come back
Another day.
Eric, Eric, catch a bus,
Don't come back
To visit us.
Eric, Eric, fly a kite,
Don't come back
Tomorrow night.
Eric, Eric, disappear,
Don't come back
For half a year.
Eric, Eric, swim a lake,
Don't come back
For heaven's sake!

Socks

My local Gents' Outfitter stocks
The latest line in snazzy socks:
Black socks, white socks,
Morning, noon and night socks,
Grey socks, green socks,
Small, large and in between socks,
Blue socks, brown socks,
Always-falling-down socks,
Orange socks, red socks,
Baby socks and bed socks;
Purple socks, pink socks,
What-would-people-think socks,
Holey socks and frayed socks,
British Empire-made socks,
Long socks, short socks,
Any-sort-of-sport socks,
Thick socks, thin socks,
And 'these-have-just-come-in' socks.

Socks with stripes and socks with spots,
Socks with stars and polka dots,
Socks for ankles, socks for knees,
Socks with twelve-month guarantees,
Socks for aunties, socks for uncles,
Socks to cure you of carbuncles,
Socks for nephews, socks for nieces,
Socks that won't show up their creases,
Socks whose colour glows fluorescent,
Socks for child or adolescent,
Socks for ladies, socks for gents,
Socks for only fifty pence.

Socks for winter, socks for autumn,
Socks with garters to support 'em.
Socks for work and socks for leisure,
Socks hand-knitted, made-to-measure,
Socks of wool and polyester,
Socks from Lincoln, Leeds and Leicester,
Socks of cotton and elastic,
Socks of paper, socks of plastic,
Socks of silk-embroidered satin,
Socks with mottoes done in Latin,
Socks for soldiers in the army,
Socks to crochet or macramé,
Socks for destinations distant,
Shrink-proof, stretch-proof, heat-resistant.

Baggy socks, brief socks,
Union Jack motif socks,
Chequered socks, tartan socks,
School or kindergarten socks,
Sensible socks, silly socks,
Frivolous and frilly socks,
Impractical socks, impossible socks,
Drip-dry machine-only-washable socks,
Bulgarian socks, Brazilian socks,
There seem to be over a million socks!

With all these socks, there's just one catch –
It's hard to find a pair that match.

Avoiding a Disturbance

The hooting of klaxons
Annoys Anglo-Saxons
In Darlington, Durham and Dover.
So when on their scooters
They don't sound their hooters,
But nonchalantly run you over.

The Bicycle

The bicycle leans against the wall,
And no one seems to care.
It clearly does no harm at all,
It therefore seems unfair
That *I* am not allowed to lean
Like that, against the wall.
It seems if I were that machine,
I'd have no cares at all.

The Birthday Cake

O why did Mavis have to make
Me such a soppy birthday cake,
With icing pink and ribbon red?
Why couldn't she have made instead
A cake of which I could be proud –
Aren't FA Cup-shaped ones allowed?

Mabel

I wonder what the matter is with Mabel?
She never seems to want to come indoors.
Is it because we're rude as we are able,
And push her underneath the kitchen table
And make her stay down there upon all fours?

An Alphabet of Horrible Habits

 A is for Albert who makes lots of noise

 B is for Bertha who bullies the boys

C is for Cuthbert who teases the cat D is for Dilys whose singing is flat

E is for Enid who's never on time F is for Freddy who's covered in slime

G is for Gilbert who never says thanks H is for Hannah who plans to rob banks

I is for Ivy who slams the front door J is for Jacob whose jokes are a bore

K is for Kenneth who won't wash his face L is for Lucy who cheats in a race

M is for
Maurice
who gobbles
his food

N is for
Nora
who runs
about nude

O is for
Olive
who treads
on your toes

P is for
Percy
who *will*
pick his nose

Q is for
Queenie
who won't tell
the truth

R is for
Rupert
who's rather
uncouth

S is for
Sibyl
who bellows
and bawls

T is for
Thomas
who scribbles
on walls

U is for
Una
who fidgets
too much

V is for
Victor
who talks
double Dutch

W is for
Wilma
who won't wipe
her feet

X is for
Xerxes
who never
is neat

Y is for
Yorick
who's vain
as can be

And Z is for
Zoe
who doesn't
love me.

French Accents

Acute, or Grave or Circumflex,
In France we use all three;
And sometimes too, Cedilla who
Is found beneath the C.

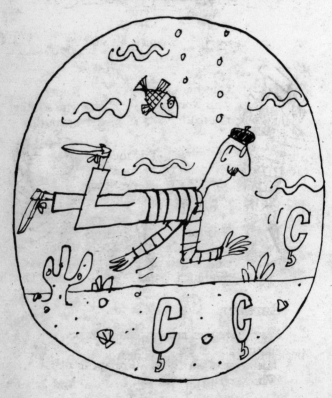

FELLOW CREATURES

Anteater

Pray, have you met my nice new pet,
An anteater is he.
There's just one hitch – I'm apt to itch
When serving up his tea.

The Grizzly Bear

The grizzly bear is horrible,
His habits quite deplorable.
He's not the sort of beast
I'd ask to tea.
The reason for my quibble is
I think *Ursus horribilis*
Looks just the sort of beast
Who might eat *me*.

The Wild Boar

The features of the porcupine
I'm glad to say are his, not mine;
Likewise the bandicoot has got
A face I do not like a lot,
And furthermore the chimpanzee
Has looks that don't appeal to me.
As for the vicious vampire bat,
I'm thankful I don't look like *that*;
And what about the octopus?
Of him I am not envious!
In fact, there is no other beast
I'd care to look like in the least;
No fellow creature comes to mind
With looks so noble and refined.
It's evident that though a boar,
I've much I should be grateful for.

The Crocodile

No cat nor dog nor bat nor frog
With fascination fills me;
Those creatures' features seem to me
To be so harmless as to be
The sort that ought to not be thought
The sort of thing that thrills me.

I much prefer the crocodile,
(You may find that alarming),
But in the croc I have a friend,
To him my love I'd like to send,
Although I know he shocks us so
With manners far from charming.

Though some may say the crocodile
Is vile, they're quite mistaken!
I like to watch him from above
When breakfasting, and I would love
To share his lair, but do not dare,
For fear I'd lose my bacon.

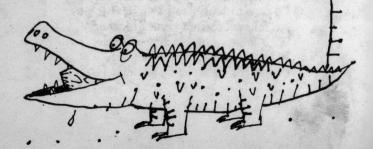

The Goldfish

The goldfish swimming in its bowl
May seem a rather lonely soul,
But better that than being in
An overcrowded sardine tin.

 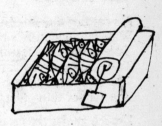

The Paradoxical Leopard

The spots the leopard's
Been allotted
Are there so leopards
Can't be spotted.

The Manatee

To test a sailor's sanity
Bring unto him a manatee
And if he finds her beautiful,
Declare him fit and dutiful.

But if he finds her hideous,
This shows he's too fastidious,
And not the sort of matelot
Who's fit to fight a battle-o.

The Orang-utan

The closest relative of man
They say, is the orang-utan;
And when I look at Grandpapa,
I realize how right they are.

PLEASE DO NOT FEED
THE ANIMALS

The Scorpion

Spiders, scorpions and mites
Are not the pleasantest of sights;
The scorpion, especially,
Does not endear itself to me.
Yet, looks aside, I must confess,
If ever I'm about to dress,
And notice one inside my shoe,
It's not as bad as failing to.

The Tortoise

The tortoise has a tendency
To live beyond his prime,
Thus letting his descendants see
How *they* will look in time.

O Rattlesnake, Rattlesnake

O Rattlesnake, Rattlesnake,
What noise does your rattle make?
O won't you please rattle
Your rattle for me?

(*So the Rattlesnake rattled its rattle.*)

O Rattlesnake, Rattlesnake,
Pray, doesn't your rattle ache?
You've rattled your rattle
Since twenty to three.

(*Still the Rattlesnake rattled its rattle.*)

O Rattlesnake, Rattlesnake,
Please no more your rattle shake.
O won't you stop rattling
Your rattle, pray do!

(*But the Rattlesnake rattled its rattle.*)

O Rattlesnake, Rattlesnake,
For you and your rattle's sake,
You'd better stop rattling
Your rattle. Thank you!

(*So the Rattlesnake bit me instead.*)

Frog

I met a frog upon a log
Who tried to tell a joke;
But sad to say his monologue
Was nothing but a croak.

My Gecko and I

I love my little gecko,
And wonder whether he
My sentiments would echo
If he could talk to me?

The Pheasant

With the looks of a peacock
And wits of an owl,
The pheasant is pleasant,
Though some say he's fowl.

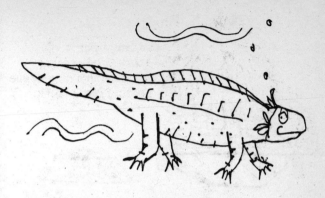

The Axolotl

The axolotl acts a little
Fishily at times.
In Mexico, some gills he'll grow,
But when in cooler climes,
Upon dry land a salamander
He may choose to be,
Though why he should and how he could
Is still not clear to me!

The Persian Cat

My pet aversion is the Persian
Of all breeds of cat,
To me this pussy seems so fussy
Over this and that.

He never stays in homes for strays in
Which his cousins dwell;
Instead this feline makes a beeline
For the Grand Hotel

And there he chooses to refuse his
Kitekat or Purr.
For he'd much sooner dine on tuna
Than eat the stuff which eight out of ten
    owners who expressed a preference *say*
    their cats prefer.

GETTING A WORD IN EDGEWAYS

Short Words

Short words that we use, such as *bee*, *bat* or *bird*,
Go under a name quite inapt and absurd;
No wonder this adjective seldom is heard,
For *monosyllabic*, I fear, is the word.

Cataract

A large waterfall
We oughtercall
A cataract,
As a matarfact.

Smith, Hacket and Grimes

I cannot say, with hand on heart,
I care for Mr Smith:
A preposition he will use
To end a sentence with.

And neither do I like a lot
Someone called Mrs Hacket.
(She puts things in parenthesis
And doesn't close the bracket.

But I can scarce put into words
How much I hate Miss Grimes.
She wants to be a poetess,
But writes appalling verses.

Grammatical Thought

Omitting an apostrophe
Or using the wrong letter –
Though neithers a catostrophe,
One really should know better.

Rhubarb, Rhubarb

'Rhubarb, rhubarb, what a lot
Of lovely rhubarb you have got
Growing in your rhubarb plot.
Rhubarb, rhubarb, rhubarb.'

'Rhubarb, rhubarb, thank you so.
Rhubarb's all I ever grow;
And I *talk* it too, you know,
Rhubarb, rhubarb, rhubarb.'

Six Tongue Twisters

Please pass the parsley, Percival,
Please pass the parsley, Percy;
The parsley, Percival, please pass,
Please, Percy, pass the parsley.

The trouble with scarecrows
Is that they *don't* scare crows,
And don't seem to care crows
Are not scared by scarecrows.

A truffle will stifle
The taste of a trifle,
But trifles won't ruffle
The triflingest truffle.

A peregrine named Peregrine
Has never grinned a grin –
Because no other peregrine
Has grinned at Peregrine.

Be true to me, beetroot, be true,
And I will too be true;
But, beetroot, if you be untrue,
I'll be untrue to you.

If a ghoul is fond of goulash,
Is the ghoul a little foolish,
Should he feel, if full of goulash,
As a ghoul he's not so ghoulish?

Superciliousness

Some say they think that 'super'
Is not the thing to say:
They say that super's silly;
Oh, supercilious they!

My Auntie

My auntie who lives in
Llanfairpwllgwyngyllgogerych-
   wyrndrobwllllantysiliogogogoch
Has asked me to stay.

But unfortunately
Llanfairpwllgwyngyllgogerych-
   wyrndrobwllllantysiliogogogoch
Is a long, long way away.

Will I ever go to
Llanfairpwllgwyngyllgogerych-
   wyrndrobwllllantysiliogogogoch?
It's difficult to say.

Etymology for Entomologists

O Longitude and Latitude,
I always get them muddled;
(I'm sure they'd be offended, though,
To think that I'm befuddled).

O Isobars and Isotherms,
Please tell me how they differ;
(For competition 'twixt the two,
I hear, could not be stiffer).

O Seraphim and Cherubim,
Don't care for one another;
(Although for me it's difficult
To tell one from the other).

O Stalagmites and Stalactites,
Whenever I peruse 'em,
Though one grows up, and one grows down,
I can't help but confuse 'em.

Longwindedness and What it Boils Down to

Would you kindly care to join me
In a game of table tennis?
(For it will be so exciting,
'Dorothea versus Dennis'.)
Can we sing *O Sole Mio*
Like the gondoliers in Venice?
Dare we watch a monster movie
All about an apelike menace?

Let's watch *King Kong*, have a ding-dong
Game of ping-pong and a sing-song.

Perissodactylate

The word *perissodactylate*
May be the sort of word you hate,
But me, I like to utter it,
And use it freely, I admit.
I've used *perissodactylate*
Three thousand and two times to date;
Now *that* makes three thousand and three,
I hardly can keep up with me.

How neatly it rolls off the tongue!
I've used the word since I was young,
In every town throughout the land,
To every local yokel, and
Perissodactylate is what
I've also said abroad a lot
When greeting foreign kings and queens.
I must find out, though, what it means.

Michael

Michael likes 'Michael',
He doesn't like 'Mike'.
He rides on a 'cycle',
And *not* on a 'bike'.
He doesn't like 'Mickey',
He doesn't like 'Mick';
Don't offer a 'bikky' –
It might make him sick.

A RECIPE FOR DISASTER

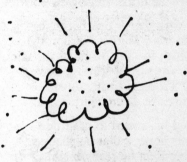

Malcolm

Let us pray for cousin Malcolm,
Smothered as he was in talcum;
He sneezed whilst seasoning his chowder
And vanished in a puff of powder.

Bruno the Sword-swallower

For years I was a follower
Of Bruno the Sword-swallower,
And to the world I endlessly would quote:
'His act is quite incredible,
He makes the sword look edible,
As inch by inch the blade goes down his throat.'

But one dark day at Scarborough,
(I'd come from Market Harborough
With friends to visit Bruno at the fair),
The rain was sort of spitting down,
He said, 'I'll do it sitting down.'
So we provided Bruno with a chair.

He gulped his sword in gratitude
And never noticed that he chewed
A bit more than he really ought to eat.
'Be careful! Mr B!' we urged.
Too late! The tip it re-emerged:
He'd riveted himself to his own seat.

Auntie Babs

Auntie Babs became besotted
With her snake, so nicely spotted,
Unaware that pets so mottled
Like to leave their keepers throttled.

Misguided Marcus

Marcus met an alligator
Half a mile from the equator;
Marcus, ever optimistic,
Said, 'This beast is not sadistic.'
Marcus even claimed the creature
'Has a kind and loving nature'.
In that case, pray tell me, Marcus,
Why have you become a carcass?

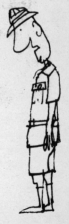

George

There was nothing George was fearing
When he went off mountaineering;
He left us amidst loud cheering,
Walking proud and tall.
Over rugged rocks he rambled,
With his life he gaily gambled,
Like a happy horse he ambled,
Not afraid at all.

But George made a fatal blunder
When he stopped a while to wonder
If the noise above was thunder –
What else could it be?
(All his life he'd lived on ranches,
Climbed up trees and swung from branches,
And not heard of avalanches.
What a tragedy!)

As George stood in meditation,
Pondering the situation,
Suddenly a sharp vibration
Filled him full of fear.
For nearby a falling boulder
Almost landed on his shoulder;
George went hotter, then went colder.
Might his end be near?

All around him great rocks rumbled,
As towards his head they tumbled.
Poor George staggered till he stumbled
And he lost his hat.

Then he started seeing double
And was soon in deeper trouble,
When a half a ton of rubble
Sadly squashed him flat.

Thus from this world George departed,
And it's left us broken-hearted;
But his trials have only started,
He is in despair.
For he once was six foot seven,
But now living up in Heaven,
He's a mere three foot eleven.
Isn't that unfair?

Charles

Charles, who always sang so purely
Met his end most prematurely,
Entertaining foreign consuls,
One of whom shot off his tonsils.

Fungus

It's most fantastic fun to be a fungus,
But no one seems to care for us a lot;
So for revenge, the mischievous among us
Look edible, but actually are not.

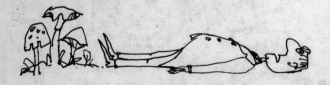

Cannibalism

Said one native to another,
As he ate up his own mother:
'How I love the female gender –
Father wasn't quite as tender.'

Jacob's Jump

When Jacob, keen to prove his fitness,
Announced he'd jump a chasm,
We gathered round this feat to witness,
With wild enthusiasm.
But Jacob's jump proved so pathetic,
Our hopes have all been banished.
No more he'll try to be athletic,
Since

d
o
w
n
t
h
e
v
o
i
d
h
e
v
a
n
i
s
h
e
d.

Bernard Ball

This is the tale of Bernard Ball,
Who liked to skip and hop,
And when he saw a likely wall,
He walked along the top.

One day, quite near the village hall,
Beside the baker's shop,
He saw a likely-looking wall,
So walked along the top.

The wall was high and Bernard Ball
Came to a sudden stop.
He lost his balance on the wall,
And tumbled from the top.

It proved to be a fatal fall
From such a drastic drop.
How tragic, falling from a wall
Whilst walking on the top.

And so we buried Bernard Ball,
Who liked to skip and hop,
But now his ghost goes to that wall,
And walks along the top.

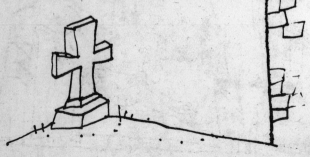

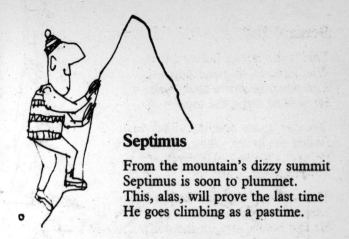

Septimus

From the mountain's dizzy summit
Septimus is soon to plummet.
This, alas, will prove the last time
He goes climbing as a pastime.

Johnny

Johnny's fatal last mistake
Was diving in a frozen lake;
He wasn't one to take advice,
And here he lies preserved in ice.

Mavis Morris

Mavis Morris was a girl
Who liked to pirouette and twirl.
One day upon a picnic, she
Whirled enthusiastically.
A hundred times she spun around –
And bore herself into the ground.

FROM HERE TO ABSURDITY

How Can I Ride?

How can I ride, you ask of me,
With so much poise and dignity?
My dear, it's Centrifugal Force
Which keeps me upright on a horse.

Mincemeat Manners

Whenever eating mincemeat pie,
I do so wish that you would try
To eat it slowly, as do I,
And savour each ingredient.
I know that children seldom do
The things their parents bid them to,
But just for once let's see if you
Can learn to be obedient!

The Loofah

The loofah feels he can't relax,
For something is amiss:
He scratches other people's backs,
But no one scratches *his*.

The Good, the Bored and the Ugly

A coachload of pupils
Get into their places –
The ones in the back seats
Make ugly grimaces.

The ones in the front seats
Are fairer of feature –
Directing the driver
And talking to Teacher.

The ones in the middle –
Halfway down the bus,
Just look bored and wonder,
'Oh, why all the fuss?'

Martha's Hair

In January Martha's hair
Was like the wild mane of a mare.
In February Martha thought
Just for a change she'd cut it short.

In March my Martha dyed it red
And stacked it high upon her head.
In April Martha changed her mind
And wore a pony tail behind.

Come May she couldn't care a fig
And shaved her head and wore a wig.
In June, when it had grown once more,
A yellow ribbon Martha wore.

And in July, like other girls,
My Martha was a mass of curls.
In August, having tired of that,
She combed it out and brushed it flat.

September saw my Martha's hair
With streaks of silver here and there.
And in October, just for fun,
On top she tied it in a bun.

November Martha chose to spend
Making her hair stand up on end.
And by December, Martha's mane
Had grown unruly once again.

The Broken-down Merry-Go-Round

Its music is silent, now it makes not a sound,
The broken-down tumbledown merry-go-round.

Its horses won't leap and its horses won't bound
On the broken-down tumbledown merry-go-round.

You won't dance and spin and you won't leave the
  ground
On the broken-down tumbledown merry-go-round.

Could ever a sadder attraction be found
Than the broken-down tumbledown merry-go-
  round?

Superfluous Surgery

He: 'One's tonsils are dispensable,
Or so the surgeons say,
So why not just be sensible
And take yours out today?

One's appendix is expendable,
It's proved beyond a doubt;
It would be most commendable
Of you to take *yours* out.'

She: 'Your brain is quite ridiculous,
As far as I can tell,
So why not be meticulous,
And take *that* out as well?'

89

Miss Evans

She dropped in for elevenses,
I heard the church bell chime
At quarter past. 'Good Heavens! Is . . .'
She muttered, 'that the time?'

I wished she'd had some previous
Engagement which was urgent,
For patenting a devious
Device to save detergent.

But no! Miss Evans couldn't care
For anything like that!
She asked me if I wouldn't care
To take her coat and hat.

She eyed my every ornament –
The cup my brother won
At some old tennis tournament.
Pray, have another bun!

I offered her Madeira cake
And coffee by the cup.
(Whenever she is near a cake
She gets the urge to sup.)

I played her some Sibelius
Upon my xylophone.
She said she favoured Delius
And scoffed a further scone.

She claimed that life's a mockery
With no one to harangue.
She claimed she liked the crockery
And took my last meringue.

She ate my salmon sandwiches
And all my apple pie.
I shook her by the hand (which is
The way to say goodbye).

She dropped in for elevenses,
But stayed to have her tea.
The thing about Miss Evans is
She 'needs the company'.

The Mermaid and the Minotaur

A mermaid met a Minotaur,
And sighed, 'Oh, how I wish
That you weren't made half like a bull,
And I half like a fish.'

The Minotaur at once replied,
'It could be worse, I vow:
Had I been made half like a fish,
And you half like a cow.'

Weather or Not

Good evening, here is the weather:
Tomorrow will be overcast,
But some fog and rain may together
Make everyone happy at last.

Some snow and some sleet are expected
At coastal resorts by the sea,
And areas mainly affected
Are those where the outbreaks will be.

But elsewhere, as soon as it's nightfall,
The sunshine will shine all day long,
And the overnight temperature *might* fall,
But sometimes I'm known to be wrong.

Old Shivermetimbers

Old Shivermetimbers, the Sea-faring Cat,
Was born on the edge of the ocean,
And his days (just to prove that the world isn't
    flat)
Are spent in perpetual motion.

Old Shivermetimbers, the Nautical Cat,
Has seen every port of the atlas;
First feline, he was, to set foot in Rabat,
A place which was hitherto catless.

Old Shivermetimbers, the Sea-faring Cat,
Has numbered as seventy-seven
The times that he's chartered the cold Kattegat
And steered by the stars up in Heaven.

Old Shivermetimbers, the Nautical Cat,
Loves the scent of the sea on his whiskers,
So it isn't surprising to hear him say that
He don't give a hoot for hibiscus.

Old Shivermetimbers, the Sea-faring Cat,
Has travelled aboard the *Queen Mary*,
Though I saw him last Saturday queuing up at
Calais, for the cross-Channel ferry.

Old Shivermetimbers, the Nautical Cat,
Has spent his whole life on the ocean,
Yet how he acquired that old admiral's hat,
I honestly haven't a notion.

How to Make Yourself Laugh

Go tickle yourself,
Go tickle yourself,
Go grow a big beard
And go tickle yourself.
If you can't grow a beard,
Just reach for the shelf
For one of these books:
(And go tickle yourself)

Not to be Taken Seriously
A Step in the Wrong Direction
The Land of Utter Nonsense